Speedy Workouts for every week of Year 3!

This CGP book is bursting with fantastic 10-Minute Workouts to improve Spelling and Vocabulary week by week in Year 3.

Each Workout includes Spelling practice matched to the National Curriculum, along with questions to expand pupils' Vocabulary and help them learn how to deal with unfamiliar words — plus a fun puzzle too!

We've even included a handy chart to track progress over the whole year, a checklist of tricky words and cut-out answers.

Published by CGP
ISBN: 978 1 78908 295 1

Editors: Emma Crighton, Harry Millican, Gabrielle Richardson and Rebecca Russell

With thanks to Juliette Green and Katharine Howell for the proofreading.

With thanks to Emily Smith for the copyright research.

Contents pages and page 74 contain public sector information licensed under the Open Government Licence v3.0. http://www.nationalarchives.gov.uk/doc/open-government-licence/version/3/

Clipart from Corel®

Printed by Elanders Ltd, Newcastle upon Tyne.

Based on the classic CGP style created by Richard Parsons.

Text, design, layout and original illustrations
© Coordination Group Publications Ltd. (CGP) 2019
All rights reserved.

**Photocopying this book is not permitted, even if you have a CLA licence.
Extra copies are available from CGP with next day delivery • 0800 1712 712 • www.cgpbooks.co.uk**

How to Use this Book

- This book contains 36 workouts. We've split them into 3 sections, one for each term, with 12 workouts each. There's roughly one workout for every week of the school year.
- Each workout is out of 12 marks and should take about 10 minutes.
- Each workout tests at least one spelling objective (from the government's programme of study) and a vocabulary topic. The vocabulary questions aim to introduce pupils to new words and expand their vocabularies.
- Pupils may not know all the vocabulary words. Encourage them to use context, or a dictionary where necessary, to work out unfamiliar words.
- Each workout ends with a fun puzzle to challenge pupils.
- The first 3 workouts in the Autumn Term test Year 2 spelling content and easier vocabulary — they're ideal for reminding pupils what they learnt in the previous year. These should be done at the start of Year 3.
- The last 6 workouts only contain Year 3 spelling content and they test harder vocabulary. They should be done at the end of Year 3.
- The other workouts contain a mix of old and new topics. As the book progresses, the tests increase in difficulty.
- Answers and a progress chart can be found at the back of the book.

The contents page will help you identify which statutory spelling requirement and vocabulary topic are being tested in each workout. You can use these to pick the workout which best suits you and the needs of your class (but remember the later in the book, the harder the workout will be, so it's best to save the workouts towards the end of the book for later in the year).

There is a tick box next to each workout on the contents page. Use this to record which tests have been attempted. You can also use the progress chart to track pupils' scores.

Contents — Autumn Term

- [ ] **Workout 1** 2
  - The 'j' sound spelt 'ge' and 'dge'
  - Spelling puzzle: The 's' sound spelt 'c'
  - Words for 'nice'

- [ ] **Workout 2** 4
  - The 'ee' sound spelt 'ey'
  - Vocabulary puzzle
  - Words to do with holidays

- [ ] **Workout 3** 6
  - Homophones and near-homophones
  - Vocabulary puzzle
  - Words to do with arguing

- [ ] **Workout 4** 8
  - Words from the Year 3 word list
  - Vocabulary puzzle
  - Words to describe jobs

- [ ] **Workout 5** 10
  - Words ending in 'y' and 'ies'
  - Spelling puzzle: Words from the Year 3 word list
  - Words to do with moving

- [ ] **Workout 6** 12
  - Adding suffixes beginning with vowel letters
  - Vocabulary puzzle
  - Words to do with size

- [ ] **Workout 7** 14
  - The 'ul' sound spelt 'le', 'el', 'al' and 'il'
  - Spelling puzzle: The 'ul' sound spelt 'le', 'el', 'al' and 'il'
  - Words to do with emotions

- [ ] **Workout 8** 16
  - Words from the Year 3 word list
  - Spelling puzzle: Words from the Year 3 word list
  - Words to do with school

- [ ] **Workout 9** 18
  - Silent letters ('wr')
  - Vocabulary puzzle
  - Words to do with winter

- [ ] **Workout 10** 20
  - The short 'i' sound spelt 'y'
  - Vocabulary puzzle
  - Words to do with the weather

- [ ] **Workout 11** 22
  - Plurals ending in 'es'
  - Spelling puzzle: Words from the Year 3 word list
  - Words to do with sport

- [ ] **Workout 12** 24
  - The short 'u' sound spelt 'ou'
  - Vocabulary puzzle
  - Noise words

Contents — Spring Term

- [ ] **Workout 1** 26
  - The suffixes '-ed', '-ing', '-er', '-est' and '-y'
  - Vocabulary puzzle
  - Words to do with nature

- [ ] **Workout 2** 28
  - Words ending in '-sure' and '-ture'
  - Spelling puzzle: Prefixes
  - Words for 'said'

- [ ] **Workout 3** 30
  - The 'or' sound spelt 'a' before 'l' and 'll'
  - Vocabulary puzzle
  - Words for 'good', 'bad' and 'okay'

- [ ] **Workout 4** 32
  - Common exception words
  - Vocabulary puzzle
  - Words to do with outer space

- [ ] **Workout 5** 34
  - Silent letters ('kn' and 'gn')
  - Spelling puzzle: The short 'u' sound spelt 'ou'
  - Adverbs

- [ ] **Workout 6** 36
  - The suffixes '-tion', '-ation', '-sion' and '-ssion'
  - Vocabulary puzzle
  - Words to do with being scared

- [ ] **Workout 7** 38
  - The short 'o' sound spelt 'a' after 'w' and 'qu'
  - Vocabulary puzzle
  - Words to do with importance

- [ ] **Workout 8** 40
  - The suffix '-ly'
  - Spelling puzzle: Words from the Year 3 word list
  - Words to do with movement

- [ ] **Workout 9** 42
  - Vowel sounds after 'w'
  - Vocabulary puzzle
  - Words to describe people

- [ ] **Workout 10** 44
  - The suffix '-ous'
  - Spelling puzzle: The short 'u' sound spelt 'ou'
  - Words to do with heat

- [ ] **Workout 11** 46
  - Homophones and near-homophones
  - Vocabulary puzzle
  - More words to do with nature

- [ ] **Workout 12** 48
  - The suffix '-ous'
  - Vocabulary puzzle
  - Words to do with feelings

Contents — Summer Term

- **Workout 1** 50
  - The 'k' and 'sh' sounds spelt 'ch'
  - Vocabulary puzzle
  - Words to describe things going well or badly

- **Workout 2** 52
  - The suffixes '-ment', '-ness', '-ful', '-less' and '-ly'
  - Vocabulary puzzle
  - Words to do with flying

- **Workout 3** 54
  - The 'g' sound spelt 'gue' and the 'k' sound spelt 'que'
  - Vocabulary puzzle
  - Words to do with eating

- **Workout 4** 56
  - The 's' sound spelt 'sc'
  - Vocabulary puzzle
  - Words for 'kind and 'unkind'

- **Workout 5** 58
  - The 'zh' sound spelt 's'
  - Spelling puzzle: The 'ey' sound spelt 'ei', 'eigh' and 'ey'
  - Words to do with exercise

- **Workout 6** 60
  - Apostrophes for possession
  - Spelling puzzle: The suffixes '-tion', '-sion', '-ssion' and '-cian'
  - Words to do with thinking

- **Workout 7** 62
  - Adding suffixes beginning with vowel letters
  - Spelling puzzle: Mixed spelling rules
  - Words to do with friendship

- **Workout 8** 64
  - Prefixes
  - Spelling puzzle: The short 'i' sound spelt 'y'
  - Words to do with history

- **Workout 9** 66
  - The suffix '-ly'
  - Vocabulary puzzle
  - Words to do with textures

- **Workout 10** 68
  - The 'g' sound spelt 'gue' and the 'k' sound spelt 'que'
  - Spelling puzzle: The 'k' and 'sh' sound spelt 'ch'
  - Words about peace and chaos

- **Workout 11** 70
  - The 'ey' sound spelt 'ei', 'eigh' and 'ey'
  - Vocabulary puzzle
  - Words to describe food

- **Workout 12** 72
  - The suffixes '-ation', '-sion' and '-cian'
  - Vocabulary puzzle
  - Words to do with geography

Tricky Words for Year 3 74

Answers 75

Progress Chart

Autumn Term: Workout 1

Spelling Practice

1. Unscramble the words in **green**.
   Use the clues in black to help you.

   it keeps food cold: firgde ....

   the opposite of small: lrage ....

   an animal with a long neck: grifafe ....

   a type of fruit: onrage ....

   a place where people exercise: mgy ....

   to avoid something: dgode ....

   6 marks

Vocabulary Questions

2. Tick **three** words that mean '**nice**'.

   ☐ lovely   ☐ excited   ☐ cheeky
   ☐ dreary   ☐ pleasant   ☐ kind

   3 marks

3. Choose words from Question 2 to replace '**nice**' in each sentence.

   There are many possible answers. Use a different word each time.

   a) My grandad made a **nice** cake. ....

   1 mark

b) The bus driver was **nice**. ....
1 mark

c) The weather is **nice** today. ....
1 mark

How did you do?   Score: [   ]

Puzzle: Picture Match

Draw lines to match each picture to the correct spelling. Then unscramble the green letters next to the correct words to find the hidden word.

1. ✏️   E   city
                               D   sity
2. 🚲   R   pencil
                               B   pensil
3. 🏙️   P   juise
                               I   juice
4. 🧃   C   bicycle
                               L   bisycle

Hidden word:

Puzzle Complete?

Autumn Term: Workout 1

Autumn Term: Workout 2

Spelling Practice

1. Unscramble the words in **brackets** to complete the sentences.

   Mina lost her front door .... (ykes)

   There is smoke coming from the .... (cmiheny)

   I fed carrots to the .... (dnoekys)

   A .... sat on my head when we were on holiday. (menoky)

   At the supermarket, I like to push the .... (torely)

   5 marks

Vocabulary Questions

2. Tick the **three** sentences that show someone is **enjoying** their holiday.

   The country is fantastic. ☐

   I've been really adventurous. ☐

   The town is dull. ☐

   The food tastes incredible. ☐

   The heat is irritating. ☐

   3 marks

3. Choose words from the box
to replace each word in **bold**.

| luggage foreign tourists explore |

The airline lost our **suitcases**. ....

I'd like to go to a **different** country. ....

I love to **walk around** new places. ....

The beach was full of **visitors**. ....

4 marks

How did you do? Score:

Puzzle: Let's Go On Holiday

Solve the clues and write the answers in the grid.
The letters in the shaded boxes spell out a holiday accessory.

1. Sometimes built from sand
2. Hot season
3. A summer shoe
4. People stay in these on holiday
5. Used to take pictures
6. Make a journey

1. C _ _ _ _
2. _ _ _ _ R
3. _ A _ _ _
4. _ _ T _ _
5. _ _ M _ _
6. _ _ V _ _

The accessory is: ....   Puzzle Complete?

Autumn Term: Workout 2

Autumn Term: Workout 3

Spelling Practice

1. Circle the correct word to complete the sentences below.

   Adil **one / won** the swimming competition.

   I can't **sea / see** very far in this fog.

   I am **too / two** small to reach the top shelf.

   Risa gave me **some / sum** cake.

   The **son / sun** will shine this weekend.

   Adeline needs a **knew / new** shirt for school.

   6 marks

Vocabulary Questions

2. Circle **three** words in the box that mean '**argued**'.

squabbled	disagreed
ran	
knew	quarrelled

   3 marks

3. Circle the word in **bold** which you think fits best.

   a) There is a **disagreement / cook** over what to have for dinner.

   1 mark

b) Kit and Harriet are **bickering / smiling** about how to make the cake.

1 mark

c) Maggie started to **know / squabble** with her brother over who had to clean the kitchen.

1 mark

How did you do?   Score:

Puzzle: Kitchen Match-Up

Use the pictures to complete the words.
Then draw lines to match each word to its definition.

   t .... b .... e   a tool to cut with

   k .... le   where you store things

   .... i .... e   heats up bread

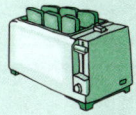   t .... t .... r   a place to eat food

   c .... b .... r ....   this boils water

Puzzle Complete?

Autumn Term: Workout 4

Spelling Practice

1. Circle the correct spelling of the words in **bold**.

   Daphne doesn't **believe / beleive** in ghosts.

   Jamal took a deep **breth / breath** and jumped into the pool.

   I'm going to **build / bild** a sandcastle.

   A **groop / group** of lions is called a pride.

   Yui swam out to the deserted **island / iland**.

   We waited ages for the train to **arive / arrive**.

   6 marks

Vocabulary Questions

2. Choose a word from the box that can replace each word in **bold**, and write it on the line.

   | satisfying   risky   thrilling |

   a) Miles is a cleaner. His job is **rewarding**. ....
   1 mark

   b) Ole is a writer. His job is **exciting**. ....
   1 mark

c) Jane is a firefighter.

   Her job is **dangerous**. ....

1 mark

3. Replace the words in **bold** with more interesting words.

   Ella is a builder who finds her job quite **easy** .... Unfortunately, she thinks her job is really **tiring** .... , and sometimes it can be **boring** ....

3 marks

How did you do? Score:

Puzzle: Construction Crossword

Use the clues to work out the building words.

Across:

1. Used to build walls
4. Using a spade
5. A safety hat

Down:

2. Something found above the fireplace
3. What you look through to see outside

Puzzle Complete?

Autumn Term: Workout 5

Spelling Practice

1. The words below are missing either '**y**' or '**ies**'. Fill in the missing letters.

    I'm going on holiday in **Jul**............ .

    James always **cop**............ my homework.

    Appl............ suncream so that you don't burn.

    Rosy **carr**............ the heavy boxes for me.

    Deema has brought a lot of **suppl**............ to share.

    5 marks

Vocabulary Questions

2. Put the words in the box in order from '**fastest**' to '**slowest**'.

    | sprint | crawl | wander | run |

    fastest ....

    ↕ ....

    ....

    slowest ....

    4 marks

3. Circle the word which has the **opposite** meaning to the word in **bold**.

Theresa **rushed** through the orchard.

ran / crept

Mohamed **strolled** to the park to meet his friends.

scurried / walked

Charlie **walked** around the shop looking for her mum.

raced / wandered

3 marks

How did you do?   Score:

Puzzle: Word List Wordsearch

Unscramble the words beginning with 's', then find and circle them in the wordsearch.

S	S	W	I	U	R	W	S
T	T	S	K	S	S	O	U
R	R	T	U	R	P	R	R
A	E	R	M	D	E	P	P
I	N	A	Z	J	C	K	R
G	G	N	B	F	I	G	I
H	T	G	C	K	A	R	S
T	H	E	H	Z	L	K	E

srtange ....

stiarght ....

surirpse ....

sertngth ....

speacil ....

Puzzle Complete?

Autumn Term: Workout 6

Spelling Practice

1. Complete the words in **bold** by adding in the missing letter or letters.

   Victor **regre**..........**ed** not going to the party

   Priya is enjoying the **begi**..........**ing** of the book.

   I had **forgo**..........**en** my gym bag.

   Troy is **garde**..........**ing** today.

   Emilia **answe**..........**ed** the phone.

   5 marks

Vocabulary Questions

2. Circle **three** words in the box that mean '**big**'.

gigantic	tiny	enormous
miniature	massive	little

   3 marks

3. **Circle** the word in **bold** which you think fits best.

   a) The city is **gigantic / miniature**, I don't have time to explore it all.

   1 mark

   b) Marta felt so **tiny / massive** when she stood next to the skyscraper.

   1 mark

c) He was **broad / slim** so the tiny shirt fit him well.

1 mark

d) The cranes in the building site were so **tall / squat** that they seemed to touch the clouds.

1 mark

How did you do?   Score:

Puzzle: Little And Large

Unscramble the bold word in each description and write it on the line. Then draw lines to match each animal to their description. Use each description once.

This animal is **ahevy**. ....

A.

This animal is **towrieng**. ....

B.

This animal is **mintiqure**. ....

C.

Puzzle Complete?

Autumn Term: Workout 7

Spelling Practice

1. Complete the words in **bold** by adding the correct ending from the box.

   | le | el | al | il |

   Lauren is a well-behaved **pup**.......... .

   Gabriel drew a perfect **circ**.......... .

   The **beet**.......... crawled across the garden.

   Mei's favourite animal is a **cam**.......... .

   Tilly and Michael sang songs from the **music**.......... .

   Fairies are **magic**.......... creatures.

   6 marks

Vocabulary Questions

2. **Circle** the word that could replace each word in **bold**.

   Harriet was **thrilled** that she came second in the race.   delighted / disappointed

   Paul was **petrified** when he saw a bear in the woods.   curious / terrified

   Sania felt **worried** about the school play.   anxious / excited

   3 marks

3. Circle the **odd one out** in each group.

a) nervous   anxious   peaceful

1 mark

b) miserable   impatient   sorrowful

1 mark

c) grateful   cheerful   joyful

1 mark

How did you do?   Score:

Puzzle: What's The Password?

Can you help? Laura has forgotten the password to get into her friend's secret clubhouse. Solve the clues and write the answers in the grid. The letters in the shaded boxes spell out the password.

1. A small pool of water on the ground

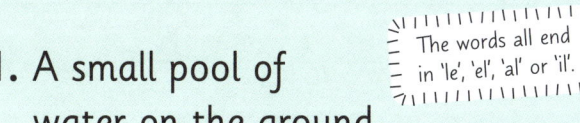
The words all end in 'le', 'el', 'al' or 'il'.

2. An underground passage

3. Nasty and unkind

4. Something you use to write

5. What you get if you win a race

6. More than a few

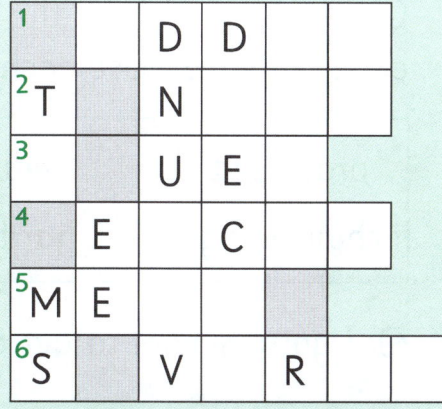

The password is:

....

Puzzle Complete?

Autumn Term: Workout 8

Spelling Practice

1. Write the correct spelling of the word in **bold** on the line.

   It's **probally** going to rain today. ....

   Jacob wants to **lern** ballet. ....

   Olivia **thort** Amina was friendly. ....

   Orhan **ansered** the phone. ....

   We're having **potatos** for lunch. ....

   I hope I have **enuff** money. ....

   6 marks

Vocabulary Questions

2. Choose a word from the box to complete each sentence. Use each word once.

organised	education
challenging	hardworking

   a) I go to school to get a good ....

   1 mark

   b) Ruby is very .... at school.

   1 mark

   c) Moheen has .... all of his files.

   1 mark

d) I struggle when homework is ....

1 mark

3. Write a sentence of your own using **one** of the words from the box in Question 2.

....

....

2 marks

How did you do?   Score:

Puzzle: Fill The Gaps

Use the clues to complete the words. The letters in the green boxes reveal something found in a classroom.

l ☐ ☐ ☐ a ☐ y = a place to read books

☐ i ☐ t ☐ ☐ = study of the past

☐ n ☐ w ☐ ☐ = the opposite of 'question'

☐ m ☐ m ☐ r = the opposite of forget

k ☐ ☐ w l ☐ ☐ e = things that you know

Hidden word: ☐ ☐ ☐ ☐ ☐

Puzzle Complete? ✓

Autumn Term: Workout 8

Autumn Term: Workout 9

Spelling Practice

1. Unscramble the words in **green**.
   Use the clues in black to help you.

   cover a present in paper: wpra ....

   not correct: wnorg ....

   draw letters and words: wrtie ....

   connects your hand to your arm: wsirt ....

   a crease in the skin: wnirkle ....

   fight someone: wesrtle ....

   6 marks

Vocabulary Questions

2. Choose words from the box to fill in the gaps in the text below. Use each word once.

   | cosy | crackled | snowflakes | frosty |

   It was Christmas Eve. Abbie looked out of her
   window at the .... fields.
   She felt .... and warm as the

fire .... in front of her.

.... began to fall outside.

She went outside and let them land on her hand.

4 marks

3. Tick **two** words that **don't** mean **cold**.

☐ chilly   ☐ mild   ☐ icy
☐ freezing   ☐ frosty   ☐ tropical

2 marks

How did you do?   Score: ☐

Puzzle: Winter Wordsearch

Unscramble the words in bold, then find them in the wordsearch.

X	S	R	B	M	P	G	S	N
H	H	B	L	I	L	Q	F	A
Y	I	O	U	K	U	Y	E	V
H	V	O	S	T	S	D	S	G
G	E	P	T	O	X	S	T	T
A	R	S	E	P	T	N	I	E
M	I	U	R	L	S	O	V	H
D	N	E	Y	W	U	W	E	T
Q	G	L	O	O	M	Y	Z	G

1. I like to go sledging when it is **sowny**.
2. I'm so cold that I'm **svihrineg**.
3. Skye feels very **ftesive** during winter.
4. The sky gets more **glomyo** at night.
5. Don't forget your coat, it's **busltery** outside.

Puzzle Complete?

Autumn Term: Workout 10

Spelling Practice

1. Circle the correct spelling of the words in **bold**.

   Yewande lifted weights at the **gym / gim**.

   It was a **mystery / mistery** who stole the toast.

   Sean likes to ride his **bicycle / bicicle** to the park.

   She only had five **mynutes / minutes** left.

   "Put that in the **byn / bin** now!" shouted Mr Gangani.

   The film was very **intresting / interesting**.

   6 marks

Vocabulary Questions

2. **Circle** the odd one out in each group.

   a) dazzling | bright | dusty

   b) breezy | blustery | wobbly

   c) soaking | damp | drenched

   3 marks

3. Complete each sentence using a word from Question 2. Use each word once.

The sentences may have more than one correct answer.

I got .... because I forgot to take my coat.

Ella put her sunglasses on because the sun was ....

Ben's hat blew away because it was a .... day.

3 marks

How did you do?   Score:

Puzzle: Weather Forecast

Use the clues to complete the words. The letters in the green boxes reveal what the weather forecast is.

u _ b _ _ l l _ = something to stop you getting wet

_ _ m _ = slightly wet

_ h _ v _ _ = what you do when you are cold

t _ _ _ d _ r = noise from a storm

_ _ _ e z _ = another word for windy

The weather forecast is:

....

Puzzle Complete? ✓

Autumn Term: Workout 11

Spelling Practice

1. Change the **bold** words into plurals by adding 'es'.

   Sometimes you need to change the word before adding 'es'.

   The buildings look **century** old. ....

   Please help me lift these **box**. ....

   I had a burger with french **fry**. ....

   When **fairy** fly, they sparkle. ....

   There are **wolf** in the forest. ....

   5 marks

Vocabulary Questions

2. Choose a word to replace each word in **bold**. Each sentence should still mean the same thing.

   She **jumped** high in the air. ....

   He **ran** faster than anyone else. ....

   She is a really **quick** runner. ....

   3 marks

3. Circle **four** words in the box that mean '**tired**'.

> exhausted   rapid   athletic   sleepy
> drowsy   speedy   weary   training

4 marks

How did you do?   Score:

Puzzle: Word List Crossword

Unscramble the words in bold to complete the crossword.

Across:

1. I had an **accdeint** on my bicycle.
2. I measure my **higeht** using a tape measure.
4. My favourite month is **Frbearuy**.

Down:

3. I like studying ancient **hstiroy**.
5. You need a lot of **kwoelndge** for the quiz.

Puzzle Complete?

Autumn Term: Workout 12

Spelling Practice

1. Add 'ou' or 'u' to complete the words in **bold** below.

   She talked in class and got in **tr..........ble**.

   They had fun blowing **b..........bbles**.

   My hair is a mess, I need to **br..........sh** it.

   France is my favourite **c..........ntry** in the world.

   Elephants have very big **tr..........nks**.

   He is so tall that he is nearly **d..........ble** my size.

   6 marks

Vocabulary Questions

2. Draw lines to **match** each **sound** with the thing that usually makes it. Use each word once.

   | tick | sizzle | crackle |

   3 marks

3. Choose words from the box to fill in the gaps in the sentences below. Use each word once.

> gurgles   growls   groaned

Snuffles the dog .... if the doorbell rings.

Alisa .... when she had to go to bed.

My stomach .... when I am hungry.

3 marks

How did you do?   Score:

Puzzle: Missing Letters

Add a letter to the box so that two words are created, like this:

F L E [A] N T S — The words created are 'flea' and 'ants'.

C L A [ ] L A Y

P A R [ ] O A L A

D R E A [ ] A G I C

F L I N [ ] R E E N

Puzzle Complete? ✓

Spring Term: Workout 1

Spelling Practice

1. Circle the correct spelling of the words in **bold** below.

   Maryam looks **happyer / happier** than Rufus.

   He was **humming / huming** his favourite song.

   Jack **cryed / cried** when his friend moved away.

   Soup is the **messiest / messyest** food.

   Her car was **shiney / shiny** when she polished it.

   5 marks

Vocabulary Questions

2. Choose words from the box to fill in the gaps in the text below. Use each word once.

   | hiking | tough | steep | loveliest |

   Last weekend, I went on a .... holiday with my friends. It was .... because the hills were so .... , but the view from the top was the .... sight I've ever seen.

   4 marks

3. Circle the odd one out in each group.

a) squawking   hooting   soaring

1 mark

b) scenery   mountain   landscape

1 mark

c) waterfall   field   meadow

1 mark

How did you do?   Score:

Puzzle: Summer Mystery

Unscramble the summer words and write them in the grid. The letters in the shaded boxes spell out an outdoor activity.

1. pssaprto
2. hlodaiy
3. baehc
4. snadacslte
5. cmapnig
6. oecan

The outdoor activity is: ....

Puzzle Complete?

Spring Term: Workout 2

Spelling Practice

1. Add '**sure**' or '**ture**' to the words in **bold** below.

   I want to **mea**............ the distance I just jumped.

   Dad moved all the **furni**............ around.

   The pirates found buried **trea**............ on the island.

   Will you hang this **pic**............ on the wall?

   I like listening to the sounds of **na**............ .

   5 marks

Vocabulary Questions

2. Sort the words in the box into words that mean '**said quietly**' and words that mean '**said loudly**'.

whispered	yelled
bellowed	murmured

   Words that mean '**said quietly**':

   ....

   ....

   Words that mean '**said loudly**':

   ....

   ....

   4 marks

3. Circle the word in **bold** which you think fits best.

We **cheered / sighed** after the knights caught the evil dragon.

The villains **roared / gossiped** in anger when they were arrested.

Ki **mumbled / shouted** her name, so I didn't hear it.

3 marks

How did you do?   Score:

Puzzle: Unlock The Secret Door

Mo is on a quest and needs your help to open the secret door.

Circle the words with the correct prefixes, then count how many times each prefix is circled. Write the numbers in the table to find the code.

unobey   unlock   unhappy

mishappy   mislock   disobey

The secret code is:

dis-	mis-	un-

Puzzle Complete?

Spring Term: Workout 3

Spelling Practice

1. Complete the words in **bold**.
   Use the pictures to help you.

   Julia kicked the **b**.......... to Kai.

   Jesse is going to **w**.......... to school.

   Sian ran into a brick **w**.......... .

   I missed an important **c**.......... from the dentist.

   Wendy wanted to **t**.......... to the manager.

   You look **sm**.......... next to him.

   6 marks

Vocabulary Questions

2. Read these sentences. Replace the words in **bold** with more interesting words. Use a different word each time.

   a) The actors in the film were **good** ....

   1 mark

b) I had a **bad** .... dream last night.

1 mark

c) Chesleigh's performance was **okay** ....

1 mark

d) Nicole is having a **good** .... time.

1 mark

3. Write a sentence of your own using **one** of the words you chose in Question 2.

....

....

2 marks

How did you do? Score:

Puzzle: Positive Pyramid

Maxwell needs your help to climb the pyramid.
If he steps on a negative (bad) word, he has to start again.
Colour in all the positive (good) words to guide him to the top.

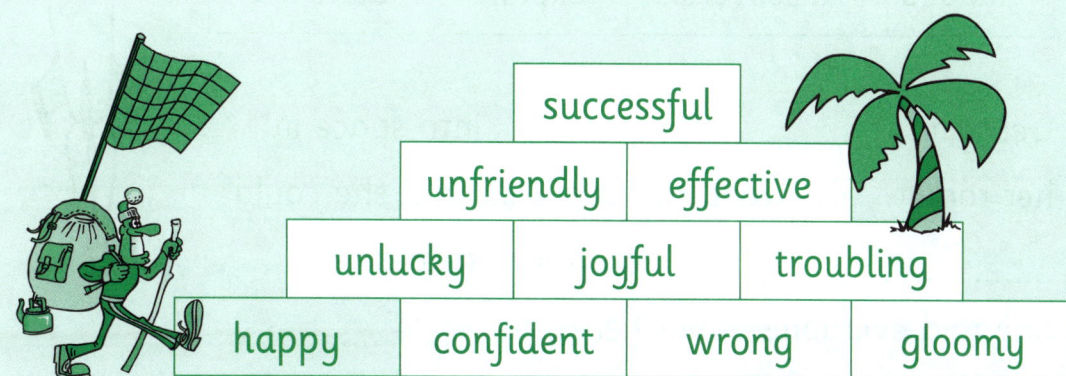

		successful		
	unfriendly	effective		
	unlucky	joyful	troubling	
happy	confident	wrong	gloomy	

Puzzle Complete?

Spring Term: Workout 4

Spelling Practice

1. Write the correct spelling of the words in **bold** on the lines.

   Lucie was eating a juicy **stayk**. ....

   My mother loves my **farthur**. ....

   Malika wants some **cloaths** to wear. ....

   Did someone just knock on the **daw**? ....

   There are a lot of **peeple** in this crowd. ....

   5 marks

Vocabulary Questions

2. Choose words from the box to fill the gaps in the sentences below. Use each word once.

   | landed   discoveries   explore   launched |

   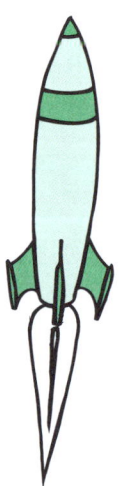

   Georgina .... into space in her rocket. She went into space so that she could .... alien landscapes. She told everyone about her .... after she .... back on Earth.

   4 marks

3. Draw lines to **match** the pairs of words that have **similar meanings**.

travel   rise   find

soar   discover   journey

How did you do?

Score: ☐ 3 marks

Puzzle: Space Crossword

Use the clues to work out the words about space.

Across:

2. A creature from another planet
4. A word that means the same as 'take off'
5. A way to travel around space
6. Someone whose job it is to go into space

Down:

1. Another word for the world
3. Something to help you see things that are far away

Across: 2. A _ I, 4. _ N H, 5. S _ _ S H _, 6. A _ _ R _ N _
Down: 3. E, 5. S, 6. P

Puzzle Complete? ✓

Spring Term: Workout 5

Spelling Practice

1. The words below are missing a silent letter. Fill in the missing letters.

   Alia hurt her ....**nee**.

   My grandma is ....**nitting** a hat.

   The rabbit ....**nawed** on the carrot.

   The ....**night** protected the castle.

   Our garden ....**nome** is called Christopher.

   5 marks

Vocabulary Questions

2. Find **two** words which mean '**happily**' and write them on the lines.

   | miserably   uneasily |
   | merrily |
   | cheerfully   gloomily |

   ....

   ....

   2 marks

3. Circle the word in **bold** which you think fits best.

   a) I cried **merrily** / **miserably** when my cat went missing.

   1 mark

b) Sue cheered **joyfully / uneasily** when her team scored.

1 mark

c) The shopkeeper shouted **calmly / angrily** at the thieves.

1 mark

d) Cara greeted me **wildly / warmly** when I arrived.

1 mark

e) "Dan lost my ball," I said **gloomily / cheerfully**.

1 mark

How did you do?　　　　　　　　　　　Score:

Puzzle: Complete The Words

Use the clues to complete the crossword.

Across:

3. When you do something bad, you get in ...
4. The opposite of old

Down:

1. Twice the amount
2. A place in the world e.g. England or India
3. Feel something with your hands

Puzzle Complete?

Spring Term: Workout 6

Spelling Practice

1. Complete the words in **bold** by adding '**tion**', '**ation**', '**sion**' or '**ssion**'.

   Mrs Simms teaches us **divi**............... in Maths.

   I need more **inform**............... before deciding.

   The wizard spilled his **po**............... all over the floor.

   After the accident, there was a lot of **confu**............... .

   Ciara asked my **permi**............... to leave.

   The husband looked at his bride in **ador**............... .

   6 marks

Vocabulary Questions

2. Circle **three** words in the text that mean '**scared**'.

   Jack was nervous as he walked into the haunted house. His friends laughed because he was frightened, but then a creak from the old floorboards startled them as well.

3 marks

Spring Term: Workout 6

3. Circle the word in **bold** which you think fits best.

Keira **screamed / whispered** when she saw a ghost in the hallway.

Thinking about monsters makes me **jingle / tremble** with fear.

Handik quickly **escaped / strolled** from the dragon's lair.

3 marks

How did you do?   Score:

Puzzle: Spooky Wordsearch

Unscramble the scary words, then find and circle your answers in the wordsearch.

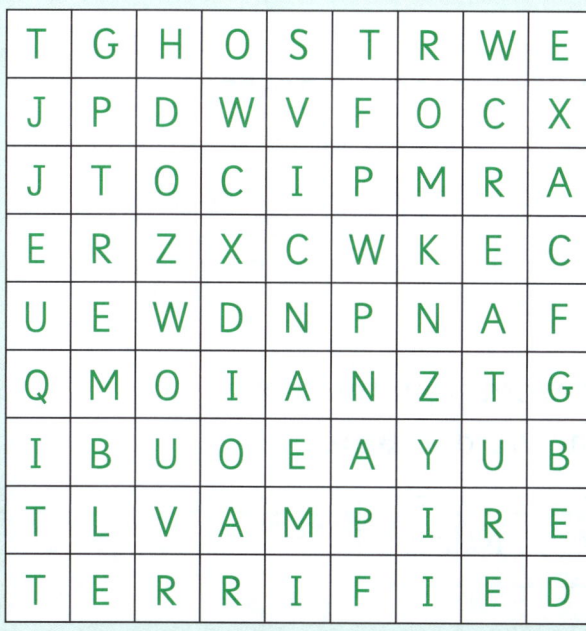

1. The **vmparie** turned into a bat.
2. The house was haunted by a **gosht**.
3. She screamed because she was **treriefid**.
4. You will **trmbele** with fear.
5. We're looking for a **cretuare**.

Puzzle Complete?

Spring Term: Workout 7

Spelling Practice

1. Unscramble the words in **green**. Use the clues in black to help you.

   desire: wnat ....

   look at: wtcah ....

   stroll: wnedar ....

   amount: qnauttiy ....

   flatten: suasqh ....

   5 marks

Vocabulary Questions

2. Circle **four** words in the box that mean '**important**'.

   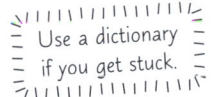
   Use a dictionary if you get stuck.

   | new | crucial | tricky | vital |
   | essential | useless | valuable | |

   4 marks

3. For each sentence, choose a word from the box with a similar meaning to the word in **bold**.

   | essential | valuable | useless |

   a) The King's crown is **expensive**. ....

   1 mark

b) A house made of chocolate is totally **worthless**.

....

1 mark

c) To build a skyscraper, it is **necessary** to have a very long ladder.

....

1 mark

How did you do?

Score:

Puzzle: Places To Live Wordsearch

Unscramble the words in bold, then find them in the wordsearch.

1. Mika lives on a **frma** in the countryside.
2. On holiday, we stayed in a **vlila**.
3. My grandma lives in a small **ctoagte**.
4. An ice house is called an **iogol**.
5. Jia lives in a top-floor **aprmtanet**.

B	F	A	R	M	K	Y	R	P
A	W	P	H	I	S	R	B	I
C	A	A	L	L	I	V	A	O
D	K	R	D	P	H	U	Y	C
C	O	T	T	A	G	E	T	S
X	T	M	B	S	W	D	I	N
M	O	E	I	I	G	L	O	O
S	Q	N	O	T	Y	I	K	P
A	V	T	Z	C	R	C	J	N

Puzzle Complete? ✓

Spring Term: Workout 8

Spelling Practice

1. Add the suffix '**ly**' to each word in **bold** to make a new word.

   Sometimes you need to change the word in bold before adding the suffix.

   The knight **final** arrived at the castle. ....

   Simon stroked the cat **gentle**. ....

   We walked into the hall very **quiet**. ....

   The clown danced around **comical**. ....

   The mean guard shouted **angry** at me. ....

   5 marks

Vocabulary Questions

2. Find **three** words in the text that describe a **movement**. Write them on the lines below.

   Charles yanked the door handle, but it wouldn't budge. He tried again, shoving the door with his body at the same time. Still nothing. It was stuck.

   ....

   ....

   ....

3 marks

3. Circle the word in **bold** which you think fits best.

The caterpillar **flapped / wriggled** across the grass.

Benji **skipped / waved** happily along the road.

Maria **shrugged / galloped** her shoulders.

You have to **drop / whisk** eggs to scramble them.

4 marks

How did you do? Score:

Puzzle: Word List Gap Fill

Use the clues to complete the words. The letters in the green boxes reveal a hidden word.

☐ ☐ ☐ a ☐ g h ☐ = the opposite of curved

f ☐ ☐ ☐ u s = well-known

☐ e d ☐ c ☐ e = makes you better if you're ill

b i ☐ y ☐ ☐ e = it has two wheels and you can ride it

☐ ☐ b ☐ ☐ ☐ r y = the month before March

Hidden word: ☐ ☐ ☐ ☐ ☐

Puzzle Complete? ✓

Spring Term: Workout 9

Spelling Practice

1. Write the correct spelling of the words in **bold** on the lines.

   Nisha didn't say a **werd** to me today. ....

   Sam ran quickly **tewards** me. ....

   The jewel is **wurth** a lot of money. ....

   There is a **riword** for the winner. ....

   I saw a bird with a **wurm** in its beak. ....

   5 marks

Vocabulary Questions

2. Choose a word from the box that you think best describes each person, and write it on the line. Use each word once.

   | serious | likeable | cheerful | polite | sporty |

   Joe loves playing basketball. He is ....

   Marlon has lots of friends. He is ....

   Saul doesn't smile much. He is ....

   Claire has good manners. She is ....

   Shanice is always smiling. She is ....

   5 marks

3. Fill in the gaps with words that describe these people.

Helena always helps other people. She is ....

Jack talks and tells stories a lot. He is ....

2 marks

How did you do?   Score:

Puzzle: Who's Who?

Unscramble the bold word in each description and write it on the line. Then draw lines to match each person to their description.

This person is **supet**. ....   A

This person is **avdetnuorus**. ....   B

This person is **hepflul**.   C

This person is **igamniaitve**. ....   D

Puzzle Complete? ✓

© CGP — not to be photocopied

Spring Term: Workout 9

Spring Term: Workout 10

Spelling Practice

1. **Circle** the correct spelling of the words in **bold**.

   Some berries are **poisonious / poisonous** to eat.

   Sometimes he can be too **serious / sereous**.

   George was **courageous / couragious** in battle.

   That is an **enormous / enormus** mountain.

   Abbie wants to be **fameous / famous**.

   5 marks

Vocabulary Questions

2. Circle **two** words in the box that mean '**hot**'.

sizzling	mild	scorching
damp	burnt	gusty

   2 marks

3. Write a sentence of your own using **one** of the words from Question 2.

   ....

   ....

   2 marks

4. Choose words from the box to fill the gaps in
   the sentences below. Use each word once.

   | baked | thirsty | blazing |

   Jemima had run out of water, so she was

   .... The sun was

   .... as it shone down

   and .... the sand below.

   3 marks

   How did you do?   Score:

   ## Puzzle: Complete The Word Grid

   Unscramble the bold words and write them in the grid. The letters in the shaded boxes spell out a secret word to do with the desert.

   1. Golnar likes riding **dubole**-decker buses.
   2. Try not to get in **tourble** when you go out.
   3. Italy is my favourite **cotnury**.
   4. I haven't got **eonugh** cake for everyone.
   5. I am very close to all of my **couniss**.

   The hidden word is:

   ....

   Puzzle Complete?

Spring Term: Workout 11

Spelling Practice

1. Write the correct spelling of the words in **bold** on the lines.

   "It's not **fayre**," groaned Nisha. ....

   My sunflower has **grone** really tall. ....

   Sam won a gold **medle** in athletics. ....

   I can hardly see through the **myst**. ....

   The horse shook its **mayn**. ....

   5 marks

Vocabulary Questions

2. Draw lines to **match** the pairs of words that have **similar meanings**.

   pretty   vast   calm

   spacious   peaceful   picturesque

   3 marks

3. **Circle** the word in **bold** that you think fits best.

   a) Lisa often climbs in **mountainous / sleek** areas.

   1 mark

b) Ethan was impressed with the **ordinary / stunning** landscape.

1 mark

c) The meadow looked much more **dreary / vibrant** once the colourful flowers were in bloom.

1 mark

d) The **extensive / cramped** gardens stretched out ahead of Hannah as she admired the view.

1 mark

How did you do?

Score:

Puzzle: Outdoors Wordsearch

Unscramble the words and find them in the wordsearch.

Z	U	W	B	U	L	B	S	B
M	G	I	S	U	J	V	U	F
O	M	L	I	Z	U	Y	P	L
U	Y	D	R	I	D	A	M	O
N	J	L	M	E	A	D	O	W
T	N	I	M	U	W	Y	A	E
A	P	F	P	W	M	Q	D	R
I	E	E	W	B	R	S	E	Z
N	A	T	U	R	A	L	W	V

1. Alex climbed the **mnuotain** slowly.
2. Ruth bent down to smell the pretty **flweor**.
3. We both like to run through the **mdaeow**.
4. The outdoors is full of **willidfe**.
5. The **nautral** world is fascinating.
6. They planted flower **blbus** in the soil.

Puzzle Complete?

Spring Term: Workout 12

Spelling Practice

1. Circle the correct spelling of the words in **bold** below.

   Serena has a **serious / serius** frown.

   My sister is a **famous / famus** rock climber.

   Rory looked **glamourous / glamorous** last night.

   We had to fight a **hidious / hideous** monster.

   Vijay made an **outrageous / outragous** request.

   5 marks

Vocabulary Questions

2. Find two words in the text that have a similar meaning to '**brave**'. Write them on the lines below.

   The fearless explorer was trapped. She needed to be very courageous if she wanted to escape.

   ....

   2 marks

3. Choose words to replace each word in **bold**. Each sentence should still mean the same thing.

   a) Tariq was **surprised** by a spider.   ....

   1 mark

   b) Monica is not **afraid** of insects.   ....

   1 mark

c) I was **eager** to climb the trees.

....
1 mark

4. Write a sentence of your own using **one** of the words you thought of in Question 3.

....

....
2 marks

How did you do?   Score: [ ]

Puzzle: Jungle Wordsearch

Unscramble the clues to do with jungle animals, then find and circle your answers in the wordsearch.

1. grolila

....

2. sanek

....

3. lzirad

....

4. mnoeky

....

5. pnaehtr

....

B	G	O	R	I	L	L	A	F
F	H	G	L	U	S	E	N	C
L	I	Z	A	R	D	S	O	P
C	H	K	M	B	K	P	G	A
L	O	C	O	F	H	A	Q	N
O	V	N	N	L	X	B	H	T
S	N	A	K	E	C	I	L	H
Q	U	W	E	I	M	N	B	E
B	K	F	Y	M	V	C	X	R

Puzzle Complete? ✓

Spring Term: Workout 12

Summer Term: Workout 1

Spelling Practice

1. Circle the correct spelling of the words in **bold** below.

   I know all the words to the song's **choruss / chorus**.

   Kira had **mashed / mached** potatoes for dinner.

   We stayed in a wooden **shalet / chalet** in France.

   My voice **eckoed / echoed** around the caves.

   Our washing **machine / masheen** flooded the kitchen.

   5 marks

Vocabulary Questions

2. Circle the word in **bold** which you think fits best.

   Maura took the hairdryer back because it was **perfect / faulty**.

   In the **confusion / calmness**, Nia dropped her books.

   He laughed at his foolish **blunder / success**.

   "There's been a **misunderstanding / correction**," apologised the receptionist.

   4 marks

3. Choose words to replace each word in **bold**.
Each sentence should still mean the same thing.

Hani accused me of eating all the ice cream, but he was **mistaken** ....

She guessed how many sweets were in the jar **accurately** ....

We will have a party to celebrate his **triumph** ....

3 marks

How did you do?   Score:

Puzzle: Error Message

Can you help? Laura has sent Tony a message, but something's gone wrong. Unscramble the green words and write them on the lines below to find out what it says.

Cgnortaluatoins on your scucses, Tony! Well done for winning the swimming race. I was ceehrnig loudly from the stands. Do you know what your next cahlelgne will be? See you soon!

....

....

Puzzle Complete? ✓

Summer Term: Workout 2

Spelling Practice

1. Complete the words in **bold** by adding a suitable suffix.

   Connie spoke to me despite her **shy**.................. .

   He felt **power**.................. to stop the villain.

   Forests are a **peace**.................. place to be.

   Prashant ran **swift**.................. to escape from the yeti.

   The twins smiled with **enjoy**.................. .

   Nico is behaving **unusual**.................. .

   6 marks

Vocabulary Questions

2. Underline **three verbs** in the text below that are to do with **flying**.

   Nisha jumped off the wall. The wind caught the huge feathers she was holding and she started to float. All of a sudden, she soared up through the clouds — she could see for miles! She laughed excitedly, swooping back down towards the ground — she'd done it!

   3 marks

3. Circle the odd one out in each group.

a) voyage | baggage | journey

1 mark

b) landing | descending | gliding

1 mark

c) cabin | airline | wing

1 mark

How did you do?   Score:

Puzzle: Jumble Jet

Unscramble the flying words and write them in the grid. The letters in the shaded boxes spell out the name of something that flies.

1. psasnegres
2. hleipocetr
3. crgao
4. praahucte
5. hvoeirng
6. cmlinbig

Hidden word: ....

Puzzle Complete?

Summer Term: Workout 3

Spelling Practice

1. Unscramble the words in **green**.
   Use the clues in black to help you.

   a place of worship: **msouqe** ....

   one-of-a-kind: **uqnuie** ....

   unclear: **vguae** ....

   a very old object: **atinuqe** ....

   body part in the mouth: **tnouge** ....

   5 marks

Vocabulary Questions

2. Sort the words and phrases in the box into the correct category.

picked at	gobbled	
	devoured	savoured

   Words that mean 'ate quickly':

   ....

   ....

   Words that mean 'ate slowly':

   ....

   ....

   4 marks

3. Circle the word in **bold** which you think fits best.

The bird **chewed / pecked** hungrily at the seeds.

Phil and Maxwell **dribbled / slurped** their drinks in the sunshine.

Sophie **gnawed / consumed** on her fingernails nervously.

3 marks

How did you do?   Score:

Puzzle: Eating Wordsearch

Unscramble the words in bold and find them in the wordsearch.

D	I	G	R	A	Z	I	N	G
E	G	M	E	U	N	X	C	U
W	P	B	I	T	T	E	R	L
G	E	A	V	O	F	I	U	P
S	U	N	K	V	G	A	N	E
S	O	Q	I	Z	Z	H	C	D
G	R	U	B	T	H	P	H	H
E	L	E	L	P	T	J	Y	B
D	N	T	O	Y	G	T	A	Z

1. Cold, **curnhcy** apples are my favourite.
2. The long **bnqaeut** table was full of food.
3. Holly **glpued** her drink thirstily.
4. **Gubr** is an informal word for food.
5. Lemons are a **btitre** fruit.
6. Cows eat by **gazrnig** on grass.

Puzzle Complete?

Summer Term: Workout 4

Spelling Practice

1. Unscramble the words in **bold**.

   Ajay's **secnetd** candle smells of cherry. ....

   The **siectnist** discovered a new planet. ....

   Mountain **sncerey** is breathtaking. ....

   The way spiders move **facsnitaes** me. ....

   I need **siscosrs** to open the packet. ....

   Jack does yoga to stretch his **mscuels**. ....

   6 marks

Vocabulary Questions

2. Circle **three** words that can be used to describe someone who is **kind**.

   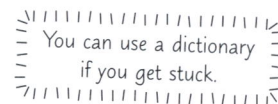
   You can use a dictionary if you get stuck.

   excitable
   considerate
   compassionate
   frightening
   sympathetic
   unfeeling
   shy

   3 marks

3. Choose words to replace the word **unkind** in each sentence. Use a different word each time.

It's **unkind** ....
to make fun of people.

"You should apologise to Raheem. You were very **unkind** .... to him," said Kim.

Everyone likes Tanya — no-one ever says **unkind** .... things about her.

3 marks

How did you do?   Score:

Puzzle: Fill The Gaps

Use the clues to complete the personality words.
The letters in the green boxes reveal a hidden word.

r _ l i _ l _ = can be trusted

f _ _ _ n d _ _ = kind and helpful

_ r e _ t _ _ e = imaginative

n e _ _ _ _ s = shy and anxious

_ _ n _ r _ u s = unselfish

Hidden word: ☐☐☐☐☐   Puzzle Complete? ✓

Summer Term: Workout 5

Spelling Practice

1. Underline the words that are spelt incorrectly and write the correct spellings on the lines.

   I wear glasses to help my vishon.   ....

   I like clothes that are cazual.   ....

   "It was my plesure," he said kindly.   ....

   6 marks

Vocabulary Questions

2. Choose a word from the box to complete each of the sentences below. Use each word once.

flexible	stretching
determination	balanced

   Gymnasts are usually very ....

   To protect your muscles, ... before you exercise is important.

   It's important to eat a .... diet.

   Athletes have a lot of ....

   4 marks

3. Use a **dictionary** to find out the meaning of the words below.

agile

....

stamina

....

2 marks

How did you do?   Score:

Puzzle: Unscramble And Search

Unscramble the words in bold and find them in the wordsearch.

1. **Tyeh** all thanked the referee after the game.
2. Tamela lifts **wiegths** at the gym every day.
3. When I am **eihgeetn**, I want to run a marathon.
4. My **ngeibohur** completed a triathlon.
5. Horseriders have to hold the **rnies** tightly.
6. Motor racing is fun if you **oeyb** the rules.

A	N	C	N	P	V	X	S	D
E	O	R	E	I	N	S	A	U
I	B	P	I	X	S	G	S	D
B	E	I	G	H	T	E	E	N
N	Y	C	H	E	H	W	T	Y
F	K	Q	B	J	G	H	H	C
E	D	L	O	T	I	L	A	Z
I	E	S	U	Y	E	H	T	I
B	U	A	R	B	W	N	O	Y

Puzzle Complete?

Summer Term: Workout 6

Spelling Practice

1. Tick the sentences below that use apostrophes correctly.

    ☐ The boys' favourite sport is hockey.

    ☐ My grandmas cake's are delicious.

    ☐ When we went camping, James's tent flooded.

    2 marks

2. Add an apostrophe to each sentence.

    Kats pens went missing last week.

    Our birds beaks are both yellow.

    I am jealous of Hamids cleverness.

    3 marks

Vocabulary Questions

3. Read the text below.

    > Sita leant closer to **marvel at** the flower. Just as she was taking a picture to **mull over** at home, the flower pulled up its roots and began to walk! Her mouth dropped open. **Convinced** it must be an **illusion**, she reached out slowly...

    What do you think the words in **bold** mean? Circle the word you think is the best match.

    a) **marvel at**   see / stare at / admire

    1 mark

b) **mull over**   think about / ignore / paint

1 mark

c) **convinced**   unsure / astonished / certain

1 mark

d) **illusion**   surprise / trick / nightmare

1 mark

4. Write a sentence of your own using **two** of the words in **bold** from Question 3.

....

....

3 marks

How did you do?   Score:

Puzzle: Complete The Words

Use the clues to help you complete the crossword.

CLUE: All the answers have similar endings.

Across:

2. Facts or data
3. Ending
5. E.g. the Prime Minister
6. Choice

Down:

1. Conversation
4. The answer to something

Puzzle Complete? ✓

Summer Term: Workout 7

Spelling Practice

1. Add in the missing letters to complete each of the words below.

   I cried at the sad film because it was **upset**............ .

   Raj is a good **listen**............, which shows that he cares.

   She has **transfer**............ to another football club.

   They're busy **creat**............ a musical masterpiece.

   Two ducks **waddl**............ to the pond where they lived.

   I am only a **begin**............ at tennis, but I like playing.

   6 marks

Vocabulary Questions

2. There are **two** words that don't belong in this group. Write them on the lines below.

affection	generosity	honesty
spitefulness	kindness	selfishness

   ....

   2 marks

3. Complete the diary entry below using the words from the box. Use each word once.

| caring   inseparable   lasting   secrets |

My best friend is extremely ....
We always help each other out and share all our
.... We're .... — we
do everything together. I hope it's a ....
friendship, and we're still best friends when we're 80.

4 marks

How did you do?   Score:

Puzzle: Correct The Advert

Can you spot the mistakes in this advert? Circle four misspelt words, then write down the correct spellings on the lines.

 FUN AND FRIENDSHIP FOR ALL

If you have a dissability that makes it hard for you to play some sports, then weelchair basketball might be just what you're looking for. It's a phisical sport, but don't let that put you off — we're all very frendly and we can't wait to meet new players!

....

....

Puzzle Complete?

Summer Term: Workout 8

Spelling Practice

1. Complete the words in **bold** by adding a prefix from the box.

   You'll need to use one prefix twice.

   | sub | ir | super | re |

   It doesn't matter anymore — it's ....**relevant**.

   Mona ....**acted** strangely when she saw the pig.

   My sister works underwater on a ....**marine**.

   Francis bought a ....**sized** bowl of chips.

   We have to use ....**headings** in our reports.

   5 marks

Vocabulary Questions

2. Find **three** words which are types of **people** and write them on the lines below.

   explorers   travels
          settlers
   invaders
          discovers
      artefacts

   ....

   ....

   ....

   3 marks

3. Circle the word in **bold** which you think fits best.

The ants **civilised / invaded** our house on 4th June.

My new **invention / empire** helps hamsters to speak.

The **traitors / relics** were moulded from Roman clay.

The historian made an exciting **discovery / rebellion**.

4 marks

How did you do?　　　　　　　　　　　Score:

Puzzle: Pool Problems

Cara is writing a poem about her holiday, but she dropped it in the pool, so some words are missing. Work out the green words to find out what her poem says.

On holiday in E〰️pt
I explored an ancient crypt
At the bottom of a 〰️amid
And found an old scr〰️

It was written in 〰️mbols
So what it said was a mystery
But I was very exc〰️d
To have found a part of 〰️tory

Puzzle Complete?

Summer Term: Workout 9

Spelling Practice

1. Circle the correct spelling of the words in **bold** below.

   She **usually / usualy** eats her lunch quite late.

   I have **truely / truly** enjoyed this day.

   Megan **gentley / gently** hugged her sister.

   Your teacher will **happily / happyly** help you.

   Nasser cried **dramatically / dramaticly**.

5 marks

Vocabulary Questions

2. Read the text below.

   > Francesca gripped the **coarse** surface of the cliff. She was nervous about hurting herself on the **jagged** rocks, and worried that the more **brittle** parts of the cliff might fall to the ground. She couldn't wait to get back home to her comfortable bed, which had **velvety** sheets.

   What do you think the words in **bold** mean?
   Circle the word you think is the best match.

   a) **coarse**   rocky / rough / solid

   1 mark

   b) **jagged**   uneven / lengthy / sandy

   1 mark

c) **brittle**   squishy / breakable / rigid

1 mark

d) **velvety**   cool / smooth / relaxing

1 mark

3. **Circle** the words which describe something that is **rough** to touch.

| bristly | sketchy | silky |
| grainy | rugged | elastic |

3 marks

How did you do?   Score:

Puzzle: Name The Pet Rock

Can you help? This pet rock has forgotten its name. To find it, fill in the gaps below. The shaded letters spell the pet rock's name.

A brush is... ☐ r ☐ s t ☐ ☐

A hedgehog is... s ☐ ☐ k ☐

A kitten is... ☐ ☐ u f ☐ ☐

A slug is... ☐ ☐ i ☐ y

A crisp is... ☐ r ☐ ☐ ☐ h ☐

The pet rock's name is:

....

Puzzle Complete?

Summer Term: Workout 10

Spelling Practice

1. Write the correct spelling of the words in **bold**.

   My team are now top of the **leugae**. ....

   Anna has a **uqniue** way of speaking. ....

   The dentist looks for **paqlue** on teeth. ....

   Lesley is suffering from **fitague**. ....

   My **tnouge** is swollen. ....

   That vase is an expensive **atinque**. ....

   6 marks

Vocabulary Questions

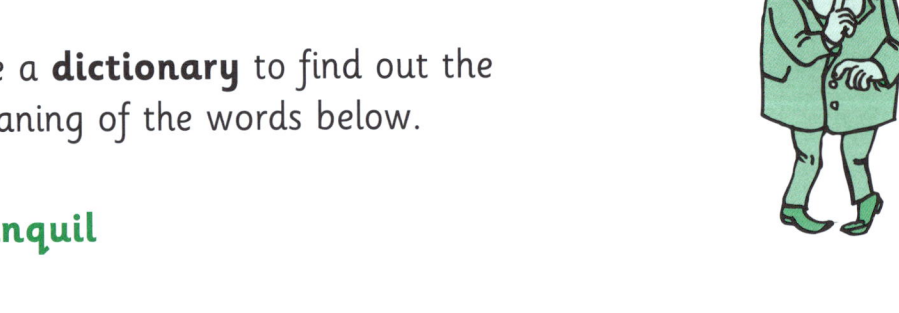

2. Use a **dictionary** to find out the meaning of the words below.

   tranquil

   ....

   turbulent

   ....

   2 marks

3. Circle the word in **bold** which you think fits best.

It was **chaotic** / **serene** as the big crowd panicked and ran away.

Her voice was **muted** / **bold** because she was nervous.

The screaming children were being **obedient** / **rowdy**.

The gentle music is very **soothing** / **stressful**.

4 marks

How did you do? Score:

Puzzle: Complete The Words

Use the clues to complete the crossword.

CLUE — All of the answers have the letters 'ch' in them.

Across:
2. A person in a story
3. A repeated sound
5. Something used to weigh down a ship

Down:
1. I get my snacks from a vending ...
2. Someone whose job is to cook
4. A group of singers

Puzzle Complete?

Summer Term : Workout 11

Spelling Practice

1. Complete the words in **bold** by adding either '**ei**', '**eigh**' or '**ey**'.

   I get on well with my next-door **n**............**bour**.

   I enjoyed filling out the **surv**............ when I had time.

   I'm nearly ....**t** years older than you.

   A bride can choose to wear a **v**............**l** at their wedding.

   I am now **w**............**ing** my pet rabbit.

   5 marks

Vocabulary Questions

2. Find **three** words which mean the same as '**tasty**' and write them on the lines below.

   appetising

   bland   edible   delicious

   revolting   flavourful

   ....

   ....

   ....

   3 marks

3. Choose words from the box to replace the words in **bold**.

   | sugary   succulent   charred   bitter |

   The chicken was nice and **juicy** .... , but the carrots were too **burnt** .... to be served. Furthermore, the lemons in the pudding were too **sour** .... , so it was not as **sweet** .... as I hoped it would be.

   4 marks

How did you do?   Score:

Puzzle: Meal Word Grid

Unscramble the food words and write them in the grid. The letters in the shaded boxes spell out the name of a food item.

1. bitert
2. flauvroufl
3. apetpising
4. astly
5. firuty

Hidden word: ....

Puzzle Complete?

Summer Term: Workout 12

Spelling Practice

1. Add in the missing letters to complete each of the words below.

   These questions test your **comprehen**............**n** skills.

   The optical **illu**............**n** was making me dizzy.

   Andy booked an eye test with the **opti**............**n**.

   Pins and needles give me a tingling **sens**............**n**.

   I called the **electri**............**n** when the power went off.

   5 marks

Vocabulary Questions

2. Write down the meaning of the **bold** words.

   You can use a dictionary if you get stuck.

   habitat

   ....

   endangered

   ....

   extinct

   ....

   3 marks

3. Choose a word from the box to complete each of the sentences. Use each word once.

> climate   solar   volcanic   geography

My parents have put .... panels on the roof of our house.

Miss Brown asked us to write about how the .... is changing.

Li enjoys learning about the .... of the world.

I saw a .... eruption when I was in Hawaii.

4 marks

How did you do?   Score:

Puzzle: Fill The Gaps

Work out the missing words and fill in the grid.

1. An ... is when the ground shakes
2. Near the sea
3. A dry, hot area
4. An area with lots of hills is ...
5. Large areas of water

	1							
1	A	R		H			K	
2	C			S		L		
3			S	E				
4	M		U	N			O	U
5		C		A				

Puzzle Complete?

Tricky Words for Year 3

Here are some tricky words — tick them off when you've learnt them.

answer ☑	famous ☑	often ☑
appear ☑	February ☑	opposite ☑
arrive ☑	fruit ☑	ordinary ☑
believe ☑	grammar ☑	popular ☑
bicycle ☑	group ☑	potatoes ☑
breath ☑	guide ☑	probably ☑
breathe ☑	heard ☑	recent ☑
build ☑	heart ☑	remember ☑
certain ☑	height ☑	sentence ☑
circle ☑	history ☑	special ☑
complete ☑	increase ☑	straight ☑
continue ☑	interest ☑	strange ☑
decide ☑	island ☑	strength ☑
different ☑	knowledge ☑	suppose ☑
difficult ☑	learn ☑	surprise ☑
early ☑	library ☑	thought ☑
earth ☑	medicine ☑	woman ☑
enough ☑	minute ☑	women ☑

Answers

Autumn Term

Workout 1 — pages 2-3

1. fridge
   large
   giraffe
   orange
   gym
   dodge
   1 mark for each correct answer

2. lovely, pleasant, kind
   1 mark for each correct answer

3. There are many possible answers.
   a) My grandad made a **lovely** cake.   1 mark
   b) The bus driver was **kind**.   1 mark
   c) The weather is **pleasant** today.   1 mark

Puzzle: Picture Match

1. R   3. E
2. C   4. I

Hidden word: **RICE**

Workout 2 — pages 4-5

1. Mina lost her front door **keys**.
   There is smoke coming from the **chimney**.
   I'm going to feed carrots to the **donkeys**.
   A **monkey** sat on my head when we were on holiday.
   At the supermarket, I like to push the **trolley**.
   1 mark for each correct answer

2. The country is fantastic.
   I've been really adventurous.
   The food tastes incredible.
   1 mark for each correct answer

3. The airline lost our **luggage**.
   I'd like to go to a **foreign** country.
   I love to **explore** new places.
   The beach was full of **tourists**.
   1 mark for each correct answer

Puzzle: Let's Go On Holiday

1. CA**S**TLE   4. H**O**TELS
2. S**U**MMER   5. CA**M**ERA
3. SA**N**DAL   6. **T**RAVEL

The accessory is: **SUNHAT**

Workout 3 — pages 6-7

1. won
   see
   too
   some
   sun
   new
   1 mark for each correct answer

2. squabbled, disagreed, quarrelled
   1 mark for each correct answer

3. a) disagreement   1 mark   c) squabble   1 mark
   b) bickering   1 mark

Puzzle: Kitchen Match-Up

t**ab**le — a place to eat food
ke**tt**le — this boils water
kn**if**e — a tool to cut with
t**oas**ter — heats up bread
cu**pboa**rd — where you store things

Workout 4 — pages 8-9

1. believe
   breath
   build
   group
   island
   arrive
   1 mark for each correct answer

2. a) satisfying   1 mark   c) risky   1 mark
   b) thrilling   1 mark

3. There are many possible answers.
   E.g. Ella is a builder who finds her job quite **simple**. Unfortunately, she thinks her job is really **exhausting**, and sometimes it can be **dull**.
   1 mark for each correct answer

Puzzle: Construction Crossword

Across: Down:
1. BRICKS   2. CHIMNEY
4. DIGGING   3. WINDOW
5. HELMET

Workout 5 — pages 10-11

1. Jul**y**
   cop**ies**
   Appl**y**
   car**ries**
   suppl**ies**
   1 mark for each correct answer

© CGP — not to be photocopied

Answers

2. Fastest: **sprint**
   run
   wander
   Slowest: **crawl**
   1 mark for each answer in the correct order

3. crept
   scurried
   raced
   1 mark for each correct answer

Puzzle: Word List Wordsearch

The words are:
strange
straight
surprise
strength
special

S	S	W	I	U	R	W	S
T	T	S	K	S	S	O	U
R	R	T	U	R	P	R	R
A	E	R	M	D	E	P	P
I	N	A	Z	J	C	K	R
G	G	N	B	F	I	G	I
H	T	G	C	K	A	R	S
T	H	E	H	Z	L	K	E

Workout 6 — pages 12-13

1. regre**tt**ed
   begi**nn**ing
   forgo**tt**en
   garde**n**ing
   answe**r**ed
   1 mark for each correct answer

2. gigantic, enormous, massive
   1 mark for each correct answer

3. a) gigantic   1 mark   c) slim   1 mark
   b) tiny   1 mark   d) tall   1 mark

Puzzle: Little And Large

This animal is **heavy**. — **C**

This animal is **towering**. — **A**

This animal is **miniature**. — **B**

Workout 7 — pages 14-15

1. pup**il**
   circ**le**
   beet**le**
   cam**el**
   music**al**
   magic**al**
   1 mark for each correct answer

2. delighted
   terrified
   anxious
   1 mark for each correct answer

3. a) peaceful   1 mark   c) grateful   1 mark
   b) impatient 1 mark

Puzzle: What's The Password?

1. **P**UDDLE   4. **P**ENCIL
2. **T**UNNEL   5. MEDA**L**
3. C**R**UEL   6. S**E**VERAL

The password is: **PURPLE**

Workout 8 — pages 16-17

1. probably
   learn
   thought
   answered
   potatoes
   enough
   1 mark for each correct answer

2. a) I go to school to get a good **education**.   1 mark
   b) Ruby is very **hardworking** at school.   1 mark
   c) Moheen has **organised**
      all of his files.   1 mark
   d) I struggle when homework
      is **challenging**.   1 mark

3. There are many possible answers.
   E.g. Yasmina is more **organised** than I am.
   2 marks for any sensible answer

Puzzle: Fill The Gaps

li**b**rary
hist**o**ry
answer
remember
knowle**d**ge

Hidden word: **board**

Answers

76

© CGP — not to be photocopied

Workout 9 — pages 18-19

1. wrap
    wrong
    write
    wrist
    wrinkle
    wrestle
    1 mark for each correct answer

2. It was Christmas Eve. Abbie looked out of her window at the **frosty** fields. She felt **cosy** and warm as the fire **crackled** in front of her. **Snowflakes** began to fall outside. She went outside and let them land on her hand.
    1 mark for each correct answer

3. mild, tropical
    1 mark for each correct answer

Puzzle: Winter Wordsearch

The words are:
1. snowy
2. shivering
3. festive
4. gloomy
5. blustery

X	S	R	B	M	P	G	S	N
H	H	B	L	I	L	Q	F	A
Y	I	O	U	K	U	Y	E	V
H	V	O	S	T	S	D	S	G
G	E	P	T	O	X	S	T	T
A	R	S	E	P	T	N	I	E
M	I	U	R	L	S	O	V	H
D	N	E	Y	W	U	W	E	T
Q	G	L	O	O	M	Y	Z	G

Workout 10 — pages 20-21

1. gym
    mystery
    bicycle
    minutes
    bin
    interesting
    1 mark for each correct answer

2. a) dusty   c) damp
    b) wobbly
    1 mark for each correct answer

3. There are many possible answers.
    E.g. I got **drenched** because I forgot to take my coat.
    E.g. Ella put her sunglasses on because the sun was **dazzling**.
    E.g. Ben's hat blew away because it was a **blustery** day.
    1 mark for each correct answer

Puzzle: Weather Forecast

umbr**r**ella
d**a**mp
sh**i**ver
thu**n**der
breez**y**

The weather forecast is: **rainy**

Workout 11 — pages 22-23

1. centuries
    boxes
    fries
    fairies
    wolves
    1 mark for each correct answer

2. There are many possible answers.
    E.g. jumped — leaped
    E.g. ran — sprinted
    E.g. quick — swift
    1 mark for each correct answer

3. exhausted, drowsy, weary, sleepy
    1 mark for each correct answer

Puzzle: Word List Crossword

Across:
1. ACCIDENT
2. HEIGHT
4. FEBRUARY

Down:
3. HISTORY
5. KNOWLEDGE

Workout 12 — pages 24-25

1. tr**ou**ble
    b**u**bbles
    br**u**sh
    c**ou**ntry
    tr**u**nks
    d**ou**ble
    1 mark for each correct answer

Answers

2.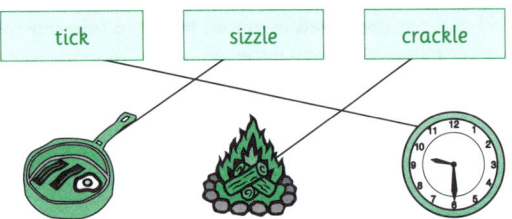

1 mark for each correct answer

3. Snuffles the dog **growls** if the doorbell rings.
   Alisa **groaned** when she had to go to bed.
   My stomach **gurgles** when I am hungry.
   1 mark for each correct answer

Puzzle: Missing Letters

The correct letters are:

P (CLA**P**, **P**LAY)
K (PAR**K**, **K**OALA)
M (DREA**M**, **M**AGIC)
G (FLIN**G**, **G**REEN)

Spring Term

Workout 1 — pages 26-27

1. happier
   humming
   cried
   messiest
   shiny
   1 mark for each correct answer

2. Last weekend, I went on a **hiking** holiday with my friends. It was **tough** because the hills were so **steep**, but the view from the top was the **loveliest** sight I've ever seen.
   1 mark for each correct answer

3. a) soaring 1 mark   c) waterfall 1 mark
   b) mountain 1 mark

Puzzle: Summer Mystery

1. **P**ASSPORT   4. S**A**NDCASTLE
2. HOL**I**DAY   5. CAMP**I**NG
3. BEA**C**H   6. O**C**EAN

The outdoor activity is: **PICNIC**

Workout 2 — pages 28-29

1. mea**sure**
   furni**ture**
   trea**sure**
   pic**ture**
   na**ture**
   1 mark for each correct answer

2. Words that mean 'said quietly' —
   whispered, murmured
   Words that mean 'said loudly' —
   bellowed, yelled
   1 mark for each correct answer

3. cheered, roared, mumbled
   1 mark for each correct answer

Puzzle: Unlock The Secret Door

The correct words are unlock, unhappy and disobey.

The secret code is: **102**

Workout 3 — pages 30-31

1. b**all**
   w**alk**
   w**all**
   c**all**
   t**alk**
   sm**all**
   1 mark for each correct answer

2. There are many possible answers.
   a) E.g. The actors in the film were **brilliant**
      1 mark
   b) E.g. I had a **terrible** dream last night.
      1 mark
   c) E.g. Chesleigh's performance was **average**.
      1 mark
   d) E.g. Nicole is having a **fantastic** time.
      1 mark

3. There are many possible answers.
   E.g. I think my new haircut looks **fantastic**.
   2 marks for any sensible answer

Puzzle: Positive Pyramid

The positive words are: confident, joyful, effective, successful.

Workout 4 — pages 32-33

1. steak
   father
   clothes
   door
   people
   1 mark for each correct answer

2. Georgina **launched** into space in her rocket. She went into space so that she could **explore** alien landscapes. She told everyone about her **discoveries** after she **landed** back on Earth.
   1 mark for each correct answer

3. travel — journey
   rise — soar
   find — discover
   1 mark for each correct answer

Puzzle: Space Crossword

Across:
2. ALIEN
4. LAUNCH
5. SPACESHIP
6. ASTRONAUT

Down:
1. EARTH
3. TELESCOPE

Workout 5 — pages 34-35

1. **k**nee
   knitting
   gnawed
   knight
   gnome
   1 mark for each correct answer

2. merrily, cheerfully
   1 mark for each correct answer

3. a) miserably   1 mark
   b) joyfully   1 mark
   c) angrily   1 mark
   d) warmly   1 mark
   e) gloomily   1 mark

Puzzle: Complete The Words

Across:
3. TROUBLE
4. YOUNG

Down:
1. DOUBLE
2. COUNTRY
3. TOUCH

Workout 6 — pages 36-37

1. divi**sion**
   inform**ation**
   po**tion**
   confu**sion**
   permi**ssion**
   ador**ation**
   1 mark for each correct answer

2. nervous
   frightened
   startled
   1 mark for each correct answer

3. screamed, tremble, escaped
   1 mark for each correct answer

Puzzle: Spooky Wordsearch

The words are:
1. vampire   2. ghost
3. terrified   4. tremble
5. creature

T	G	H	O	S	T	R	W	E
J	P	D	W	V	F	O	C	X
J	T	O	C	I	P	M	R	A
E	T	Z	X	C	W	K	E	C
U	E	W	D	N	P	N	A	F
Q	M	O	I	A	N	Z	T	G
I	B	U	O	E	A	Y	U	B
T	L	V	A	M	P	I	R	E
T	E	R	R	I	F	I	E	D

Workout 7 — pages 38-39

1. want
   watch
   wander
   quantity
   squash
   1 mark for each correct answer

2. crucial, valuable, essential, vital
   1 mark for each correct answer

3. a) The King's crown is **valuable**.   1 mark
   b) A house made of chocolate is totally **useless**.
      1 mark
   c) To build a skyscraper, it is **essential** to have a very long ladder.   1 mark

Puzzle: Places To Live Wordsearch

The words are:
1. farm
2. villa
3. cottage
4. igloo
5. apartment

B	F	A	R	M	K	Y	R	P
A	W	P	H	I	S	R	B	I
C	A	A	L	L	I	V	A	O
D	K	R	D	P	H	U	Y	C
C	O	T	T	A	G	E	T	S
X	T	M	B	S	W	D	I	N
M	O	E	I	I	G	L	O	O
S	Q	N	O	T	Y	I	K	P
A	V	T	Z	C	R	C	J	N

Workout 8 — pages 40-41

1. finally
    gently
    quietly
    comically
    angrily
    1 mark for each correct answer

2. yanked, budge, shoving
    1 mark for each correct answer

3. wriggled
    skipped
    shrugged
    whisk
    1 mark for each correct answer

Puzzle: Fill The Gaps

straight
fa**m**ous
med**i**cine
bicyc**l**e
F**e**bruary

The letters in the shaded boxes spell **smile**.

Workout 9 — pages 42-43

1. word
    towards
    worth
    reward
    worm
    1 mark for each correct answer

2. Joe loves playing basketball. He is **sporty**.
    Marlon has lots of friends. He is **likeable**.
    Saul doesn't smile much. He is **serious**.
    Claire has good manners. She is **polite**.
    Shanice is always smiling. She is **cheerful**.
    1 mark for each correct answer

3. There are many possible answers.
    E.g. Helena always helps other people. She is **helpful**.
    Jack talks and tells stories a lot. He is **chatty**.
    1 mark for each correct answer

Puzzle: Who's Who?

upset — D
adventurous — A
helpful — B
imaginative — C

Workout 10 — pages 44-45

1. poisonous
    serious
    courageous
    enormous
    famous
    1 mark for each correct answer

2. sizzling, scorching
    1 mark for each correct answer

3. There are many possible answers.
    E.g. I left my food in the oven, so it ended up getting **burnt**.
    2 marks for any sensible answer

4. Jemima had run out of water, so she was **thirsty**. The sun was **blazing** as it shone down and **baked** the sand below.
    1 mark for each correct answer

Puzzle: Complete The Word Grid

DOUBLE
TRO**U**BLE
COU**N**TRY
ENOUGH
COUSIN**S**

The hidden words is: **DUNES**

Workout 11 — pages 46-47

1. fair
    grown
    medal
    mist
    mane
    1 mark for each correct answer

Answers

2. pretty — picturesque
vast — spacious
calm — peaceful
1 mark for each correct answer

3. a) mountainous 1 mark   c) vibrant 1 mark
   b) stunning 1 mark   d) extensive 1 mark

Puzzle: Outdoors Wordsearch

1. mountain   2. flower
3. meadow   4. wildlife
5. natural   6. bulbs

Z	U	W	B	U	L	B	S	B
M	G	I	S	U	J	V	U	F
O	M	L	I	Z	U	Y	P	L
U	Y	D	R	I	D	A	M	O
N	J	L	M	E	A	D	O	W
T	N	I	M	U	W	Y	A	E
A	P	F	P	W	M	Q	D	R
I	E	E	W	B	R	S	E	Z
N	A	T	U	R	A	L	W	V

Workout 12 — pages 48-49

1. serious
   famous
   glamorous
   hideous
   outrageous
   1 mark for each correct answer

2. fearless, courageous
   1 mark for each correct answer

3. There are many possible answers.
   a) e.g. shocked 1 mark   c) e.g. keen 1 mark
   b) e.g. terrified 1 mark

4. There are many possible answers.
   E.g. I feel **fortunate** to be able to go to school.
   2 marks for any sensible answer

Puzzle: Jungle Wordsearch

The words are:
1. gorilla   4. monkey
2. snake   5. panther
3. lizard

B	G	O	R	I	L	L	A	F
F	H	G	L	U	S	E	N	C
L	I	Z	A	R	D	S	O	P
C	H	K	M	B	K	P	G	A
L	O	C	O	F	H	A	Q	N
O	V	N	N	L	X	B	H	T
S	N	A	K	E	C	I	L	H
Q	U	W	E	I	M	N	B	E
B	K	F	Y	M	V	C	X	R

Summer Term

Workout 1 — pages 50-51

1. chorus
   mashed
   chalet
   echoed
   machine
   1 mark for each correct answer

2. faulty
   confusion
   blunder
   misunderstanding
   1 mark for each correct answer

3. Hani accused me of eating all the ice cream, but he was **wrong**.
   She guessed how many sweets were in the jar **correctly**.
   We will have a party to celebrate his **victory**.
   1 mark for each correct answer

Puzzle: Error Message

The words are:
Congratulations
success
cheering
challenge

© CGP — not to be photocopied

81

Answers

Workout 2 — pages 52-53

1. shy**ness**
   power**less**
   peace**ful**
   swif**tly**
   enjoy**ment**
   unusual**ly**
   1 mark for each correct answer

2. float
   soared
   swooping
   1 mark for each correct answer

3. a) baggage 1 mark   c) airline 1 mark
   b) gliding 1 mark

Puzzle: Jumble Jet

1. **p**assengers   2. helicopter
3. car**g**o   4. parachu**t**e
5. h**o**vering   6. climbi**n**g

Hidden word: **PIGEON**

Workout 3 — pages 54-55

1. mosque
   unique
   vague
   antique
   tongue
   1 mark for each correct answer

2. Words that mean 'ate quickly' — devoured, gobbled
   Words that mean 'ate slowly' — picked at, savoured
   1 mark for each correct answer

3. pecked
   slurped
   gnawed
   1 mark for each correct answer

Puzzle: Eating Wordsearch

The words are:
1. crunchy   4. grub
2. banquet   5. bitter
3. gulped   6. grazing

D	I	G	R	A	Z	I	N	G
E	G	M	E	U	N	X	C	U
W	P	B	I	T	T	E	R	L
G	E	A	V	O	F	I	U	P
S	U	N	K	V	G	A	N	E
S	O	Q	I	Z	Z	H	C	D
G	R	U	B	T	H	P	H	H
E	L	E	L	P	T	J	Y	B
D	N	T	O	Y	G	T	A	Z

Workout 4 — pages 56-57

1. scented
   scientist
   scenery
   fascinates
   scissors
   muscles
   1 mark for each correct answer

2. considerate, compassionate, sympathetic
   1 mark for each correct answer

3. There are many possible answers.
   E.g. It's **inconsiderate** to make fun of people.
   E.g. "You should apologise to Raheem. You were very **rude** to him," said Kim.
   E.g. Everyone likes Tanya — no-one ever says **mean** things about her.
   1 mark for each correct answer

Puzzle: Fill The Gaps

relia**b**le
f**r**iendly
cre**a**tive
ner**v**ous
g**e**nerous

Hidden word: **brave**

Answers

Workout 5 — pages 58-59

1. I wear glasses to help my vishon. — vision
   I like clothes that are cazual. — casual
   "It was my plesure," he said kindly. — pleasure
   1 mark for each correctly underlined answer and 1 mark for each correct spelling

2. Gymnasts are usually very **flexible**.
   To protect your muscles, **stretching** before you exercise is important.
   It's important to eat a **balanced** diet.
   Athletes have a lot of **determination**.
   1 mark for each correct answer.

3. There are many possible answers.
   agile — e.g. lively and quick
   stamina — e.g. endurance
   1 mark for each correct answer

Puzzle: Unscramble And Search

The words are:
1. they   2. weights
3. eighteen   4. neighbour
5. reins   6. obey

A	N	C	N	P	V	X	S	D
E	O	R	E	I	N	S	A	U
I	B	P	I	X	S	G	S	D
B	E	I	G	H	T	E	E	N
N	Y	C	H	E	H	W	T	Y
F	K	Q	B	J	G	H	H	C
E	D	L	O	T	I	L	A	Z
I	E	S	U	Y	E	H	T	I
B	U	A	R	B	W	N	O	Y

Workout 6 — pages 60-61

1. The boys' favourite sport is hockey.
   When we went camping, James's tent flooded.
   1 mark for each correct answer

2. Kat's pens went missing last week.
   Our birds' beaks are both yellow.
   I am jealous of Hamid's cleverness.
   1 mark for each correct answer

3. a) admire   1 mark   c) certain   1 mark
   b) think about   1 mark d) trick   1 mark

4. There are many possible answers.
   E.g. I **convinced** my parents that the paint on the walls was an **illusion**.
   1 mark for each word used correctly and 1 mark for a correct sentence

Puzzle: Complete The Words

Across:
2. INFORMATION
3. CONCLUSION
5. POLITICIAN
6. OPTION

Down:
1. DISCUSSION
4. SOLUTION

Workout 7 — pages 62-63

1. upset**ting**
   listen**er**
   transfer**red**
   creat**ing**
   waddl**ed**
   begin**ner**
   1 mark for each correct answer

2. spitefulness
   selfishness
   1 mark for each correct answer

3. My best friend is extremely **caring**. We always help each other out and share all our **secrets**. We're **inseparable** — we do everything together. I hope it's a **lasting** friendship, and we're still best friends when we're 80.
   1 mark for each correct answer

Puzzle: Correct The Advert

dissability (disability)
weelchair (wheelchair)
phisical (physical)
frendly (friendly)

Workout 8 — pages 64-65

1. **ir**relevant
   reacted
   submarine
   supersized
   subheadings
   1 mark for each correct answer

2. explorers, invaders, settlers
   1 mark for each correct answer

3. invaded
   invention
   relics
   discovery
   1 mark for each correct answer

Puzzle: Pool Problems

The words are:
Egypt
pyramid
script
symbols
excited
history

Workout 9 — pages 66-67

1. usually
   truly
   gently
   happily
   dramatically
   1 mark for each correct answer

2. a) rough   1 mark
   b) uneven   1 mark
   c) breakable   1 mark
   d) smooth   1 mark

3. bristly, grainy, rugged
   1 mark for each correct answer

Puzzle: Name The Pet Rock

bristly
sp**i**ky
fluffy
s**l**imy
crunch**y**

The pet rock's name is: **Billy**

Workout 10 — pages 68-69

1. league
   unique
   plaque
   fatigue
   tongue
   antique
   1 mark for each correct answer

2. There are many possible answers.
   tranquil — e.g. peaceful
   turbulent — e.g. unstable
   1 mark for each correct answer

3. chaotic
   muted
   rowdy
   soothing
   1 mark for each correct answer

Puzzle: Complete The Words

Across:
2. CHARACTER
3. ECHO
5. ANCHOR

Down:
1. MACHINE
2. CHEF
4. CHOIR

Workout 11 — pages 70-71

1. n**eigh**bour
   surv**ey**
   eight
   v**ei**l
   w**eigh**ing
   1 mark for each correct answer

2. appetising, delicious, flavourful
   1 mark for each correct answer

3. The chicken was nice and **succulent**, but the carrots were too **charred** to be served. Furthermore, the lemons in the pudding were too **bitter**, so it was not as **sugary** as I hoped it would be.
   1 mark for each correct answer

Puzzle: Meal Word Grid

1. bi**t**ter
2. flav**o**urful
3. **a**ppetising
4. **s**alty
5. frui**t**y

Hidden Word: **TOAST**

Workout 12 — pages 72-73

1. comprehen**sion**
   illu**sion**
   opti**cian**
   sens**ation**
   electri**cian**
   1 mark for each correct answer

2. There are many possible answers.
   habitat — e.g. where an animal lives
   endangered — e.g. at risk
   extinct — e.g. no longer existing
   1 mark for each correct answer

3. My parents have put **solar** panels on the roof of our house.
   Miss Brown asked us to write about how the **climate** is changing.
   Li enjoys learning about the **geography** of the world.
   I saw a **volcanic** eruption when I was in Hawaii.
   1 mark for each correct answer

Puzzle: Fill The Gaps

1. EARTHQUAKE
2. COASTAL
3. DESERT
4. MOUNTAINOUS
5. OCEANS